Copyright: © D. K. Turnbridge

ISBN-13: 978-1502932594

ISBN-10: 1502932598

All rights reserved. No part of this publication may be reproduced, stored in or introduced into a retrieval system, or transmitted in any form or by any means (electronic, mechanical, by photo-copying, recording or otherwise) without the prior written permission of the author.

Londoner

noun

Someone who lives in, breathes and experiences London. Every day and night.

Travelling on the tube

When commuting on the tube to work you must keep your head down and look at your smart phone or read a newspaper.

*Note it is <u>illegal</u> to make eye contact with strangers or talk to them.

London trains have plenty of space. A whole 30 cm x 30 cm square to yourself!

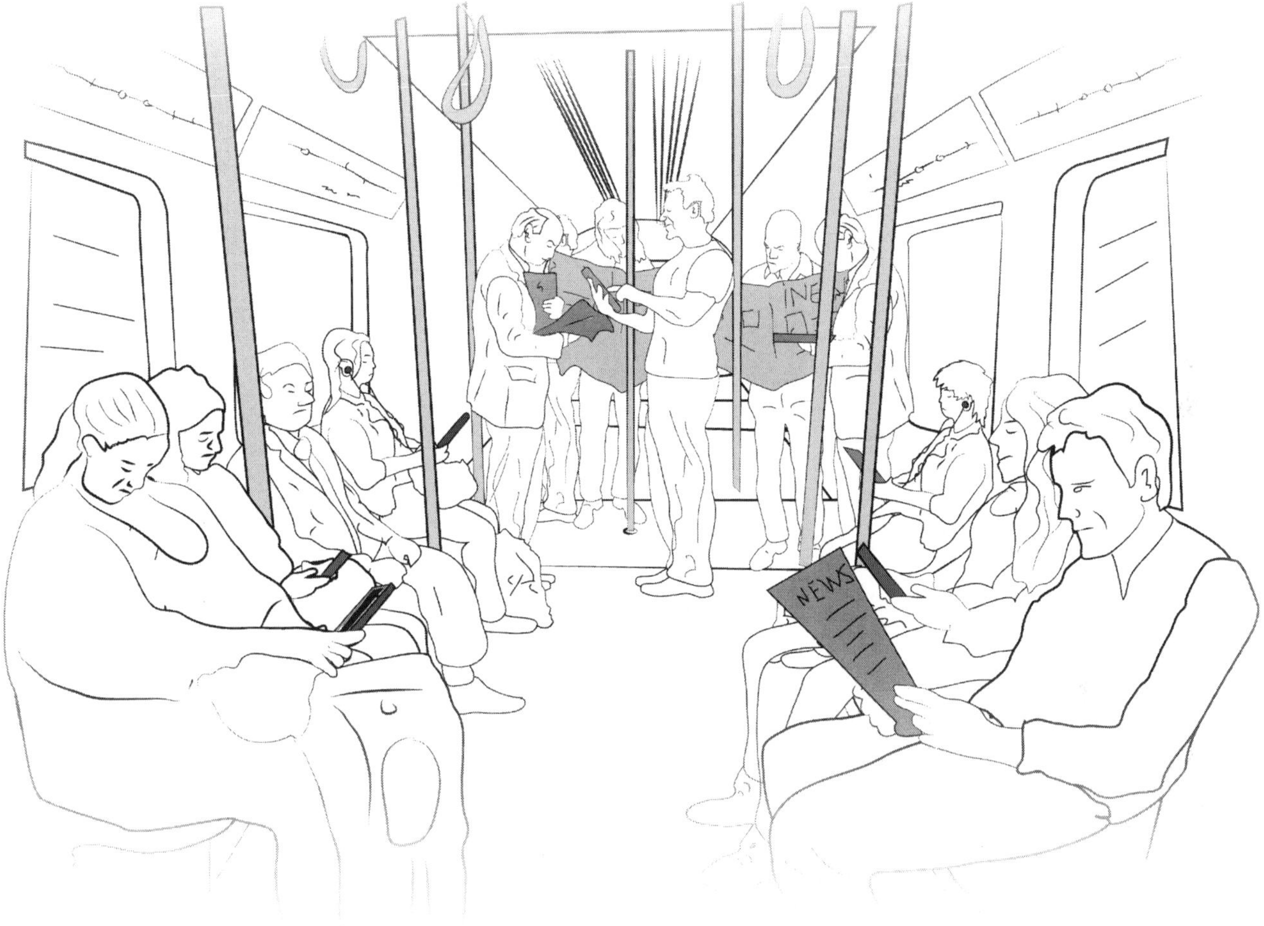
NEWS

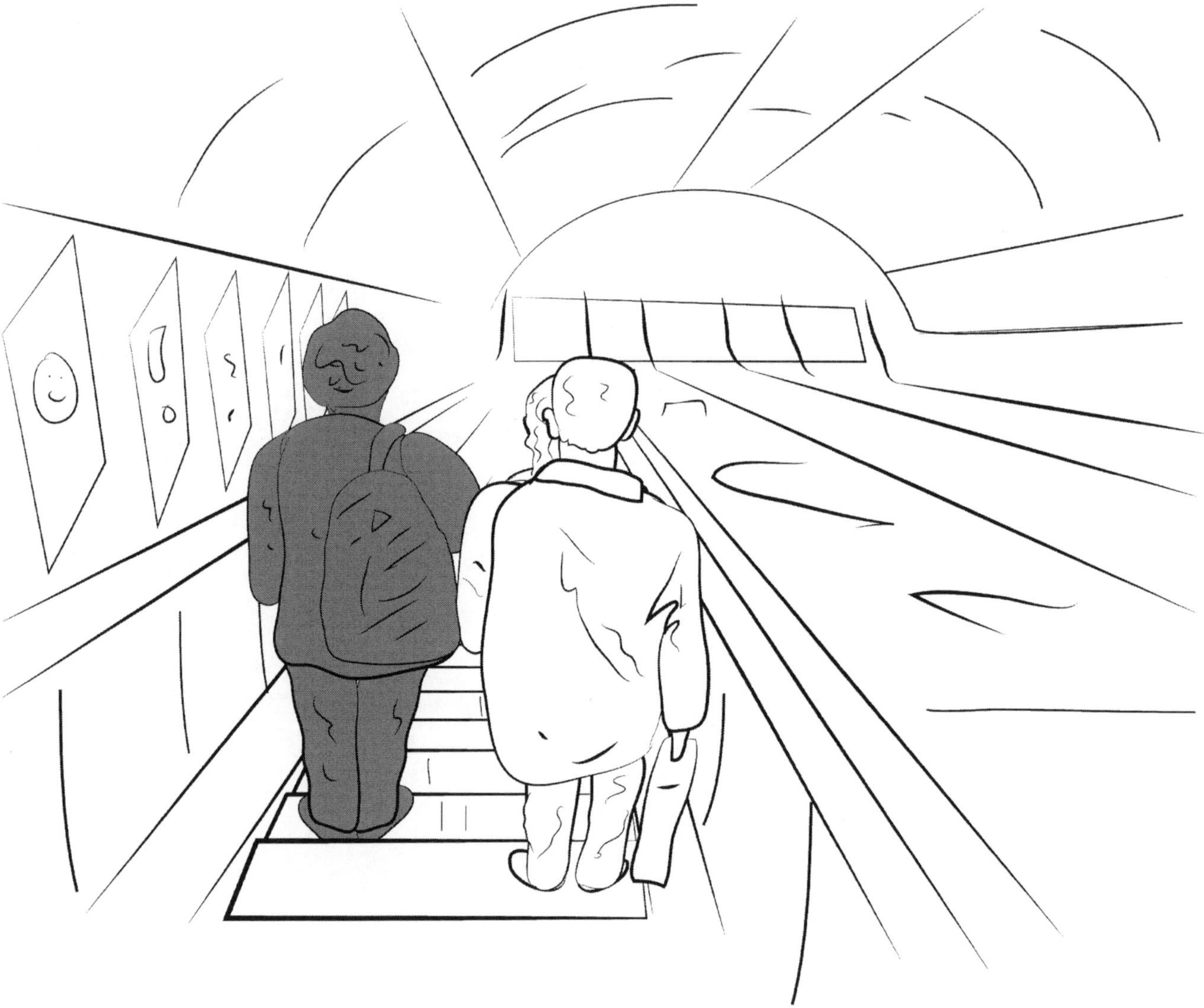

Escalators

As a London tourist your role is to stand on the left hand side of the escalator. Londoners going to work love an extra challenge in their morning commute.

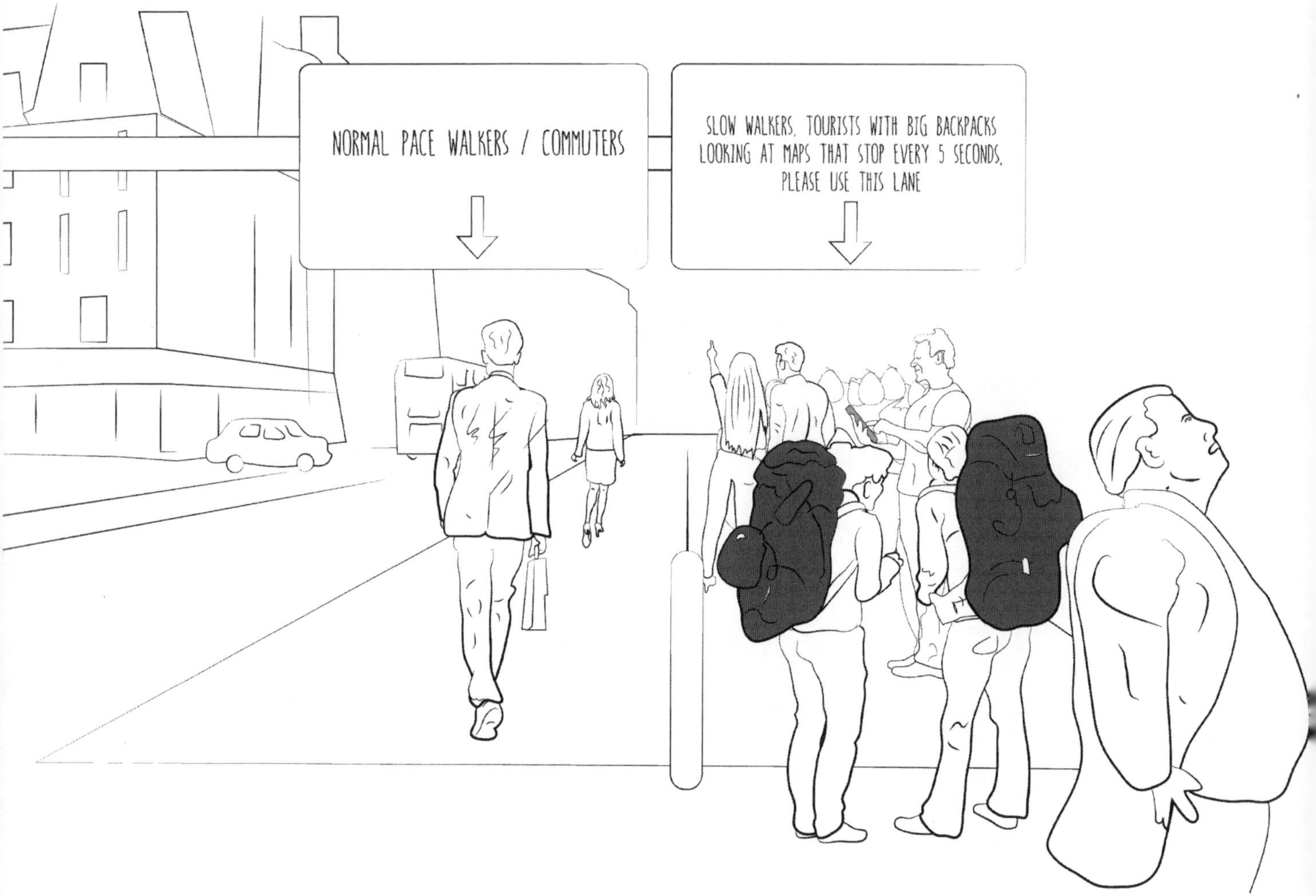
NORMAL PACE WALKERS / COMMUTERS
SLOW WALKERS, TOURISTS WITH BIG BACKPACKS LOOKING AT MAPS THAT STOP EVERY 5 SECONDS, PLEASE USE THIS LANE

Getting from A to B. Dear, slow walkers.

When walking from A to B you must set the pace at great speed.

*Coming soon 2025: Paths will be divided into two lanes.
One efficient lane for commuters and another for slow walkers, tourists with big backpacks, people who stop dead in the middle of the path every 5 seconds, large groups, etc.

GOURMET BROCCOLI ONLY

£9.99 A PIECE

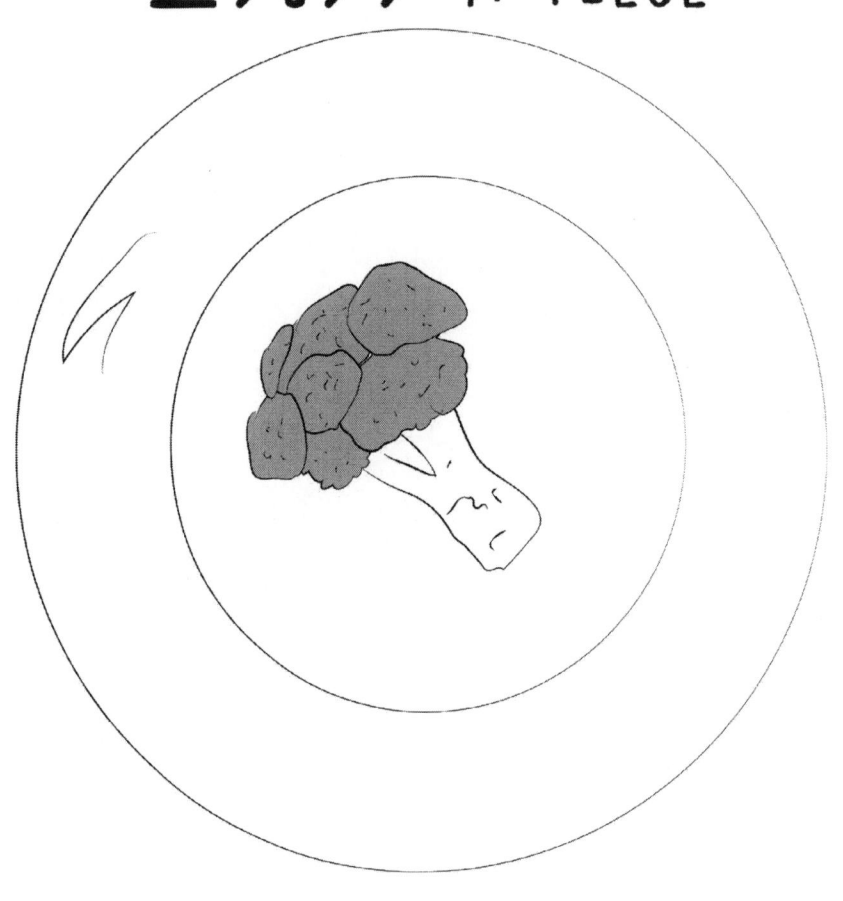

Lunchtime

It's lunchtime! Grab your favourite cuisines, portions barely enough to feed a sparrow and overpriced.

Crossing the road

A fun little game you can play in London goes by the name of 'crossing the road without getting run over'.

Because traffic comes by every 10 seconds most people just go for the jaywalking option, ending in a real life version of Frogger.

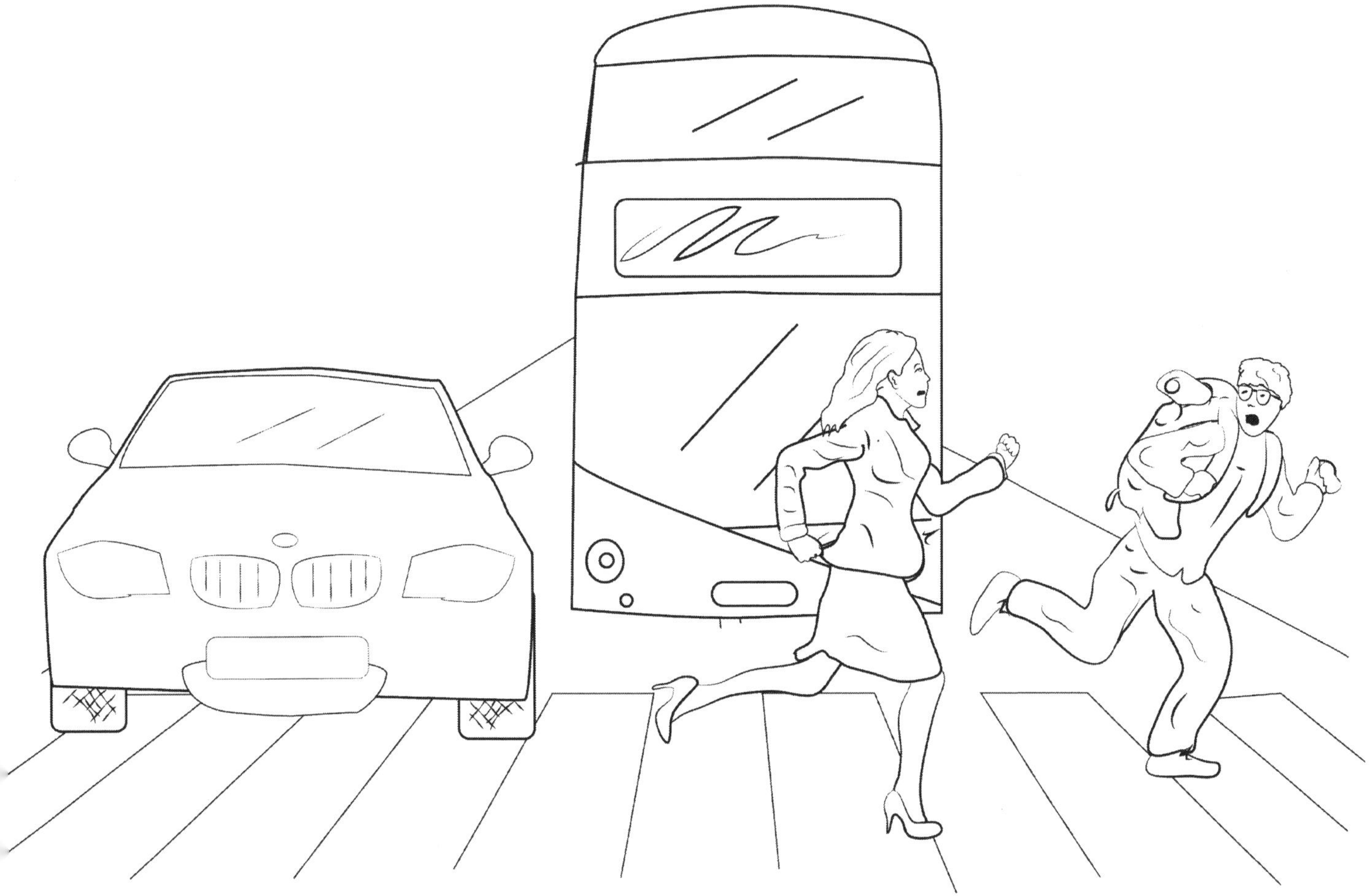

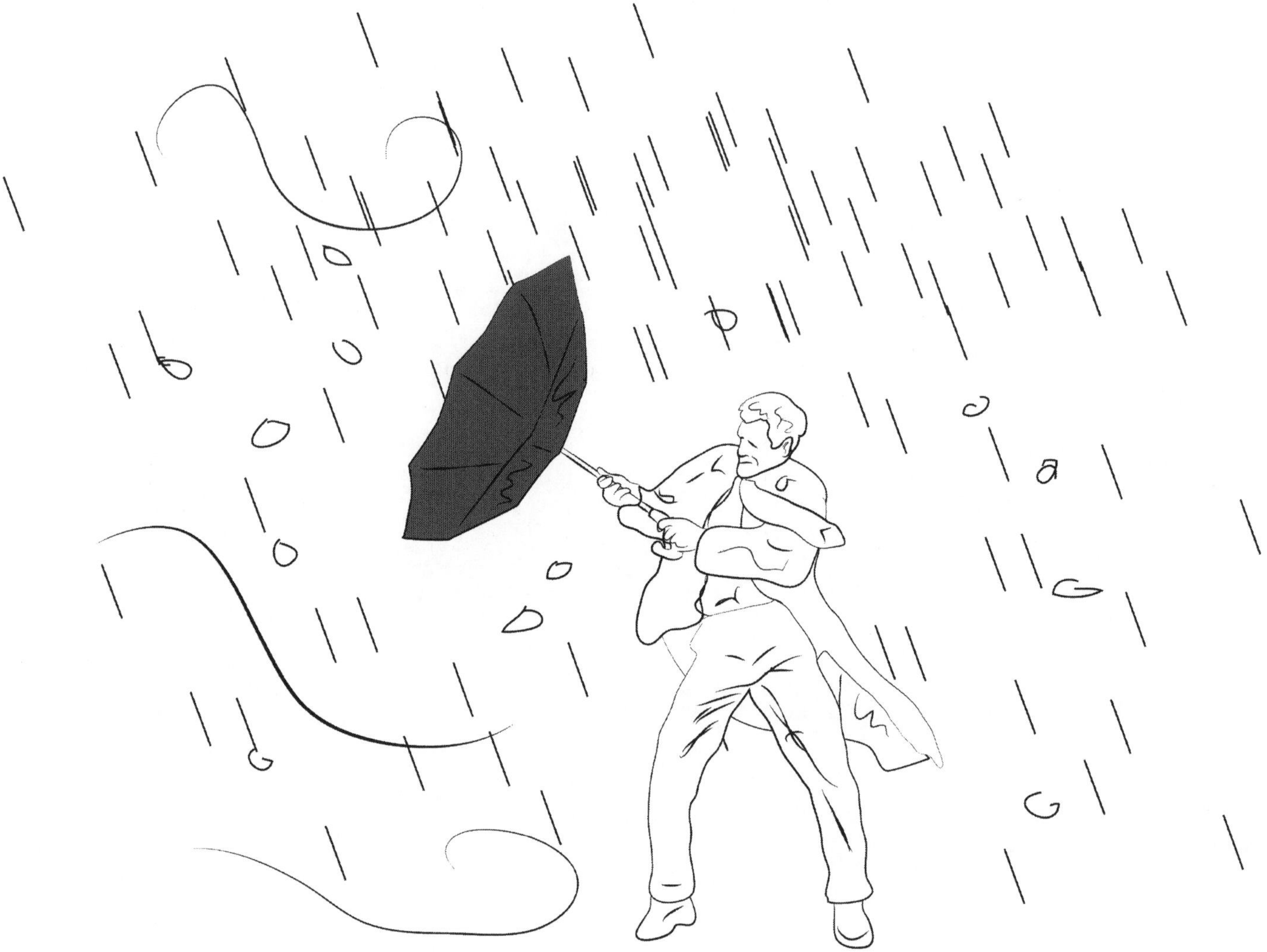

Wind and rain

A Londoner knows that the beautiful sunny weather can quickly turn to windy rain. He / she also knows to always take a brolly (although this often proves fruitless).

Names for the rain: spitting, drizzle, heaving it down, p*ssing down, tipping down, raining cats & dogs, pelting down, chucking it down.

SORRY excuse me sorry..

sorry can you repeat that?

sorry can you turn that music down?

sorry you dropped this!

Oh sorry

SORRY?!?

pardon me sorry

opps sorry!

Sorry I've just got to check this..

soorrryy

I'm ever so sorry

What is your name, sorry?

I'm so sorry

sorry!

can we have the bill, sorry?

Sorry could you errr help me here?

sorry I'm late

You can't go there sorry

ATM

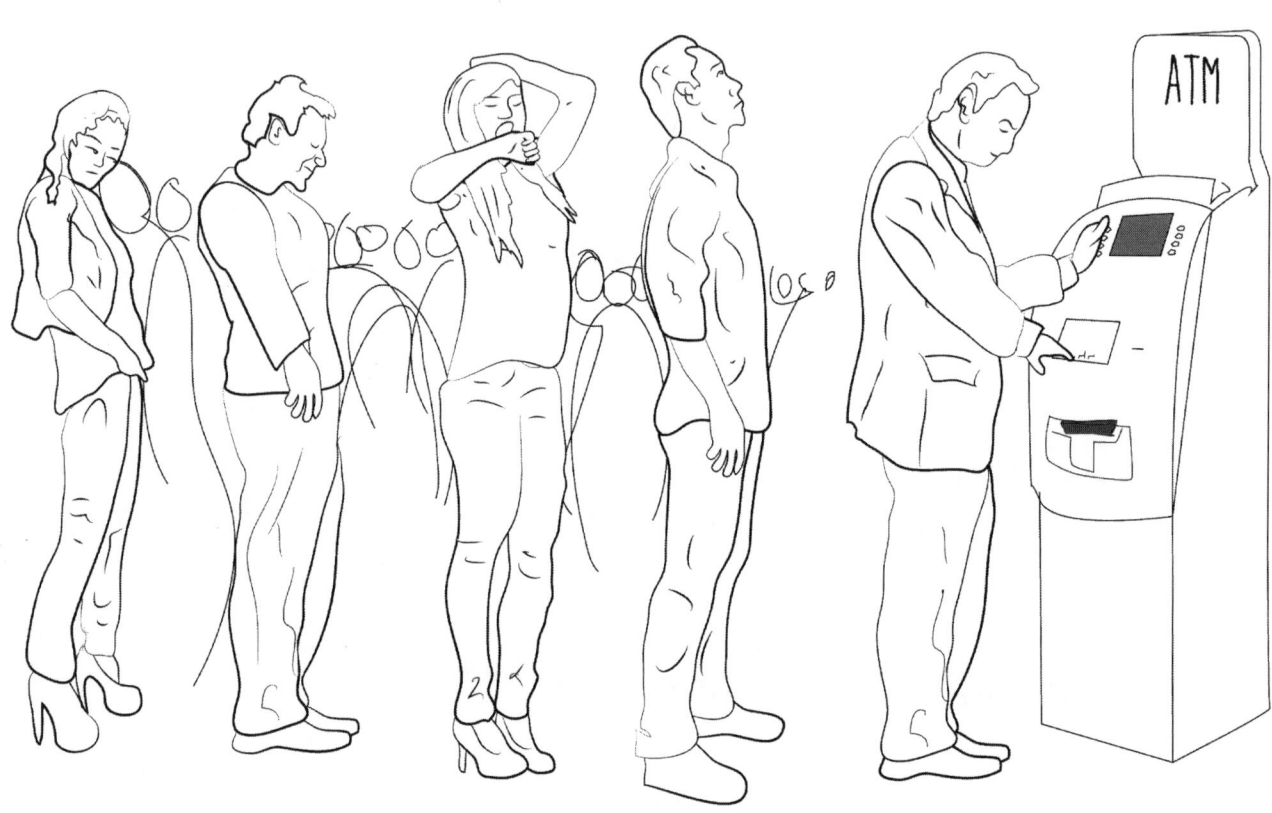

ATM queuing

There can never be enough cash machines in London. Queuing for ATMs is a popular pastime for the Londoner.

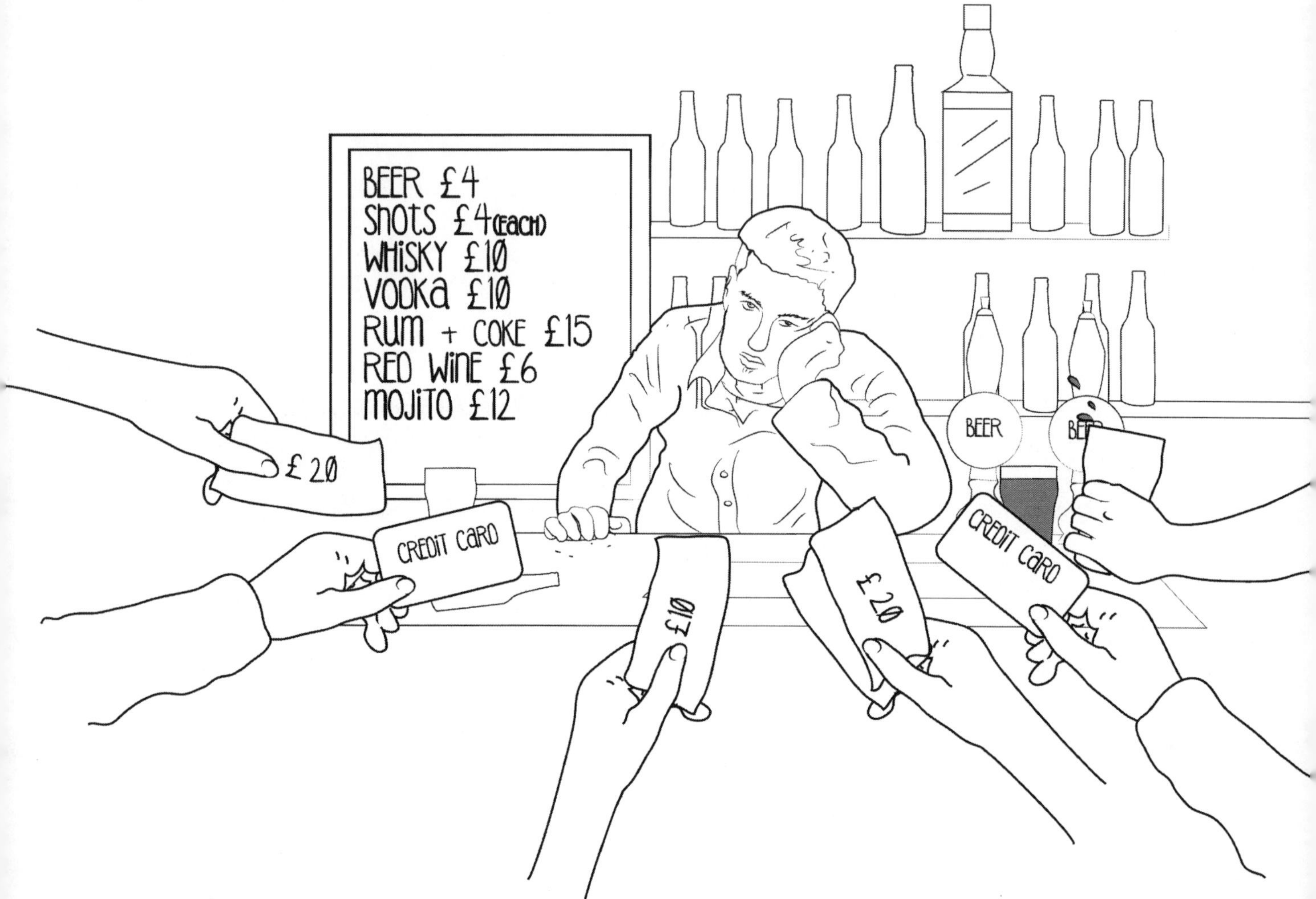
BEER £4
SHOTS £4 (EACH)
WHISKY £10
VODKA £10
RUM + COKE £15
RED WINE £6
MOJITO £12
BEER
£20
CREDIT CARD
£10
£20
CREDIT CARD

Bar/pub/club

Alcohol is the fuel of the Londoner. Without it London inhibitions kick in. This is why everyone makes a mad dash for the bar shoving each other out the way, like free money is being given away.

The price of the average pint is 4 quid. This remarkably does not phase the Londoner.

Before beer...

...After beer

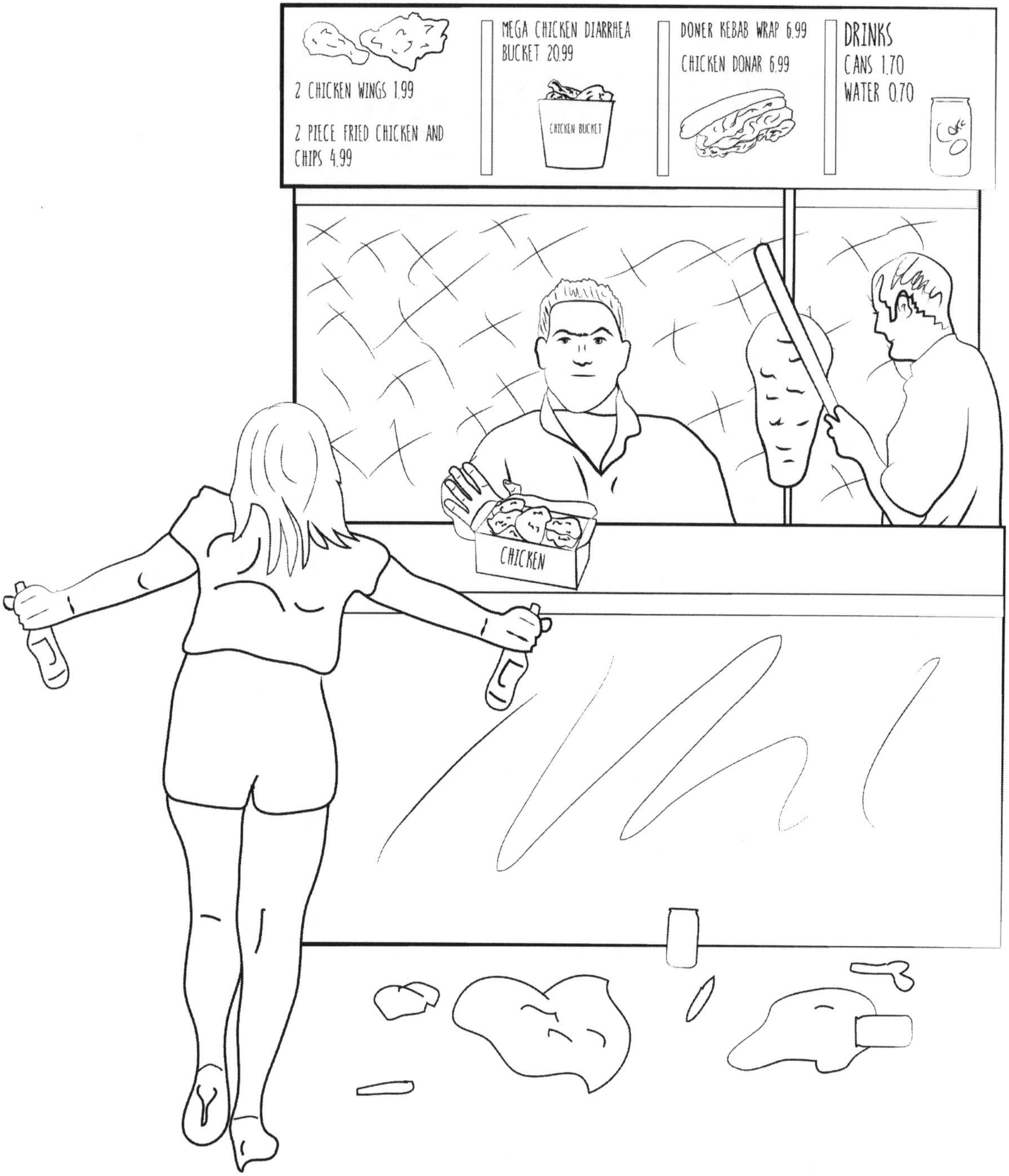
2 CHICKEN WINGS 1.99
2 PIECE FRIED CHICKEN AND CHIPS 4.99
MEGA CHICKEN DIARRHEA BUCKET 20.99
CHICKEN BUCKET
DONER KEBAB WRAP 6.99
CHICKEN DONAR 6.99
DRINKS
CANS 1.70
WATER 0.70
CHICKEN

Late night out dinner

When a Londoner fails to get laid, he/she sets off to a nearby kebab or chicken shop to cure hunger pangs.

Drunk bus

It's 3:00 am and the night out is over. The most popular transportation home by far for the Londoner is the night bus.

See if you can spot these fun characters:

- A man passed out missing his bus stop.
- Someone stuffing their mouth with fast food.
- A girl being sick.
- An angry looking man sitting on his own, playing bad music loudly from his phone / headphones.
- A loud singing group of drunk people.
- A girl crying next to her silent boyfriend.

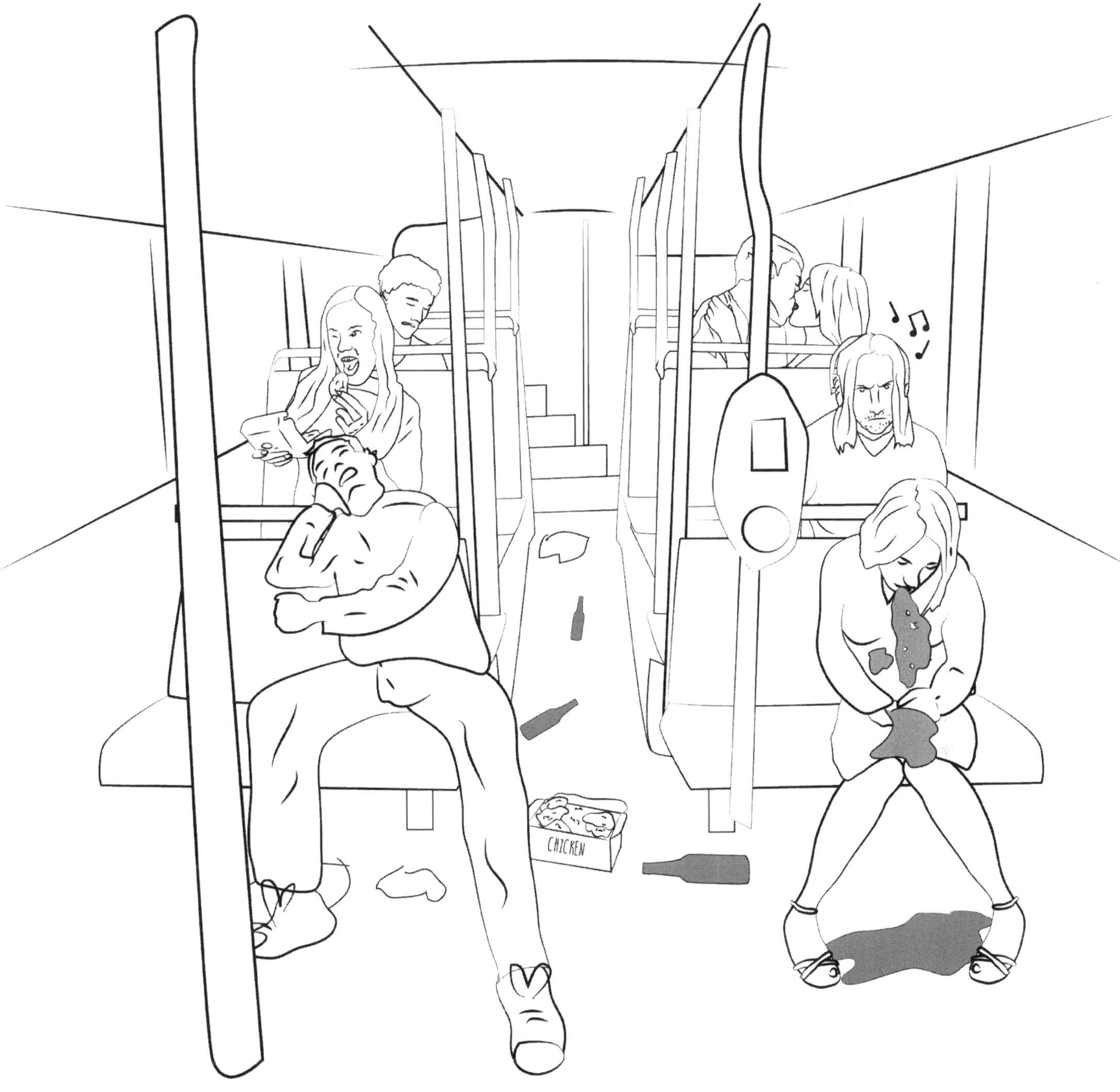
CHICKEN

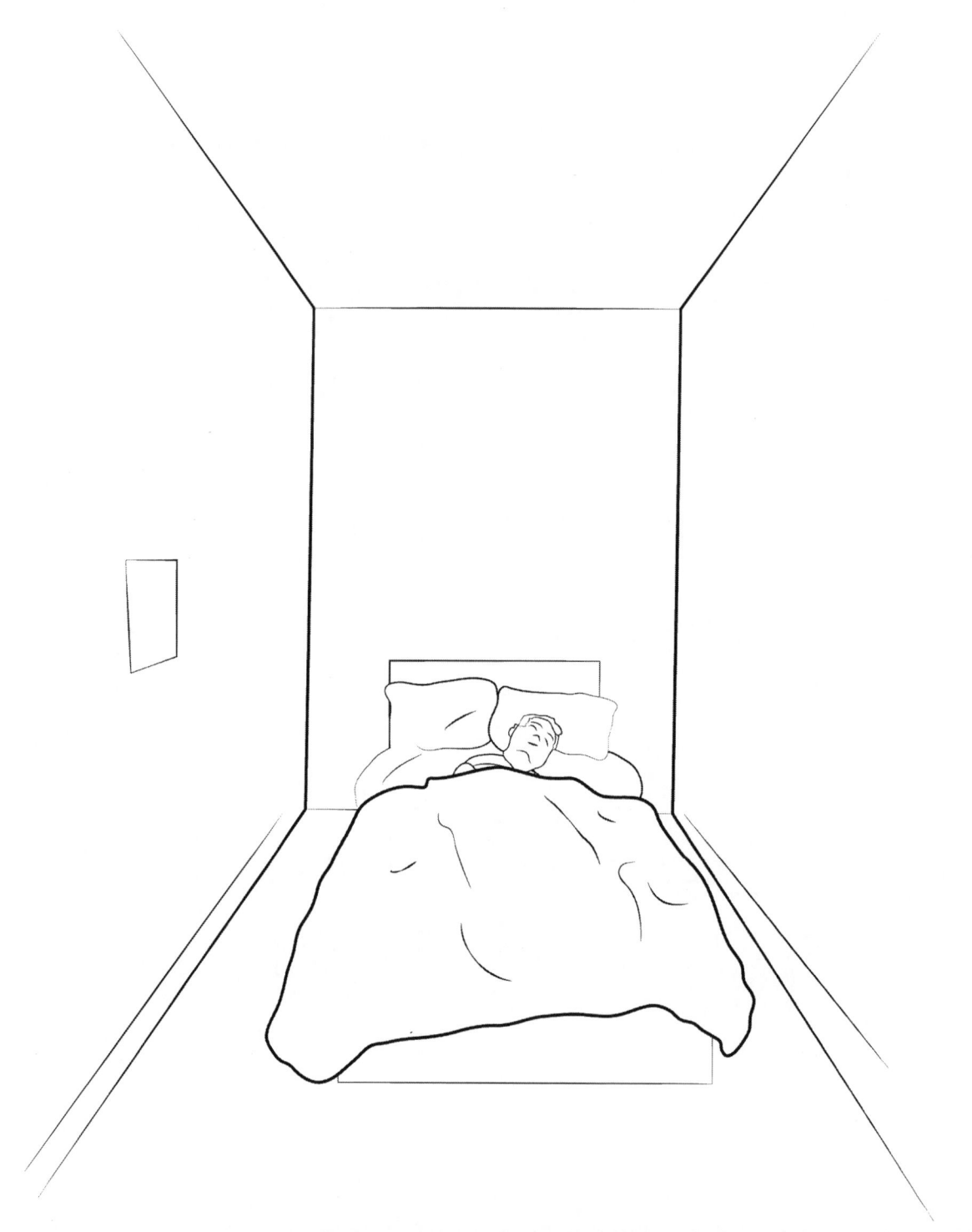

Bedroom

If English man's house is his castle. Then a Londoner's prison cell sized bedroom is his palace.

Literally.

Your rent could afford a palace anywhere else in the world.

Send your Londoner stories to: **howtobealondoner@gmail.com**

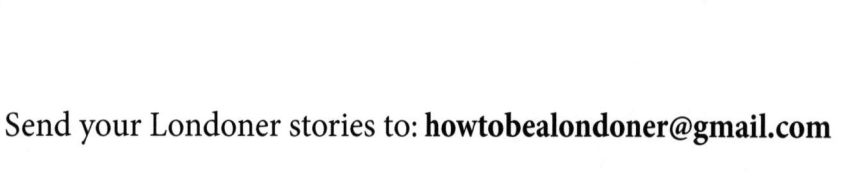

Printed in Great Britain
by Amazon.co.uk, Ltd.,
Marston Gate.